Mental Maelstrom

Lottie Dixon

BookLeaf Publishing

Presentation by *BookLeaf Publishing*

Web: www.bookleafpub.com

E-mail: info@bookleafpub.com

ISBN: 9789357213288

First edition 2023

Wish

The night breeze whispering from the distance
From the stars, I hear the mere echoes of your
name
Always haunting my thoughts and creating the
wildest dreams

Every night I,
Close my eyes to say hello
Open my eyes to say goodbye
You're the definition of a dream come true

Like someone once said, "Some good things
must have an end."
I know so much of you, but I can't say your real
to me, though
The thoughts in my head can't compare to the
mere embrace to have just ahead

I'm focused on something so unclear
I'm calling someone unknown dear
Our eyes have yet to lock, but somehow you
stole my heart This misconception of mere
perfection
Dream or reality
In the future, We shall see

Beauty

Halls of judgmental mindsets
From the womb preset to hate
Close-minded and hypocritical
Defining all odds sat one boy

Of different RACE
Of different GENDER
Of different RELIGION
Of different SEXUALITY

From there I saw, merely another
"Human"
He stood up to stare every day,
the amount of depthless persecution from his
peers
He strutted, "Heel to toe."
"Heel to toe"

A Group of his peers surrounded him
All were of merely,
Different Race
Different Gender
Different Sexuality
Different Religion

But all had one mindset in common,
"To which those aren't a custom to, tend to disagree with opening up to the belief of co-existing with something they aren't educated in. Scared of the unknown, allowing them to be close-minded and ruthless."

Attacking him brutally, I heard the cries from the center circle
"I am beautiful!"
As the kids slowly backed away from the young man, the image was more clear to me

He was covered in cuts and bruises
Torn clothes and one of his heels were broken in the assault
He looked over to me and softly spoke once again, "I am beautiful."

The color of the rainbow was radiating from his skin, and he smiles proudly up at the sky
"We are all beautiful."
He yelled over and over again

Combusting into glitter the wind had picked up, spreading his courage around the school
Sparkling for a brighter future throughout the sky

His morals and beliefs became the tea time of the world
As the sparkles in the wind blew by my ear, I heard it once more
"You are beautiful."

Ink

Ink as black as my heart
Blunt and true as my words
For that, the story is merely nonfiction
Life documented, word for word
The view from my line of sight to the paper
The mere imagery as vivid as it burns into the
mind of the reader
Captivating and dominating their mind, you see
the clear image of what lies within my mind
From where I started a just a simple hook
became a relievable memory
Just as a gust of wind opening a book
I am the inventor, and the book is the conductor,
my pen is my tool, your the receiver
But, author is my name

Gain Versus Doubt

The silence filled the cold air that surrounded her as she was running from the very toxic thoughts that plagued her mind.

The whispers of discouragement and failure lingered around her as if she was a wounded animal and the fresh scent of blood filled the air. Running as her dark brown hair hugged her pale face, every breath became harder and tiring to take. She collapsed as the plague that once consumed her mind came to reality—falling into an abyss of the fears that once were the death of her spirit. Broken at will, she only sunk deeper and deeper, drowning in the ocean of broken spirits. Her fears, taking the form of a cave with no light at the end, stairs that have no end, a pure white room with no windows or doors, and a moss-covered tombstone.

Laying there drained of all-purpose and motivation, a sound of harmonic whispers filled the air.

As if there was a festival, the air filled with roars of laughter and joyful cheers. What seemed to be a light was drawing even closer and closer to her. Hands filled below her began to push her back towards the surface. She opened her eyes as she became closer to the glistening blanket of colors that reflected onto the water's surface. As they continued to push her, their faces became clear as the water. They were people she had known, mother, brother, and close friends. Exchanging smiles and wisdom, they helped her escape the watery dungeons.

Bursting from the water's shackles, the sun's horizon greeted her with a warm embrace. She finally embraced who she was and her purpose. Flames were shooting from her back, the blaze formed in the shape of wings, and she soared into the skies. As long as her ashes remain in this world, she is immortal.

Puzzle

No Matter What
So you saw yourself cry?
Bleed?
Beg?
And Struggle?

You always tore a piece of soul and placed it into everything you do
In every stroke of a brush, words from a pen, or even your voice to the wind
Struggles come and go,
Motivation and willpower does not
Your lifestyle is a war each day
Battle well fought, don't you say?

You made it this far as open wounds become scars
Bruises grew faint
You don't carry hate in your heart
You smile, even when you know you can see the cracks within
You're like a puzzle, but with pieces missing

Each piece has its own value
Scattered your wisdom around the world

Because all the positives you place into others
lives all lead back to you
Someday all the gratitude will come, you will
see how far you came but in a full image

Claws

She was refreshing as the summer rain,
Smile like the sunrise,
Beauty of a goddess,
Keen eyes,
Silver tongue,
But those claws

She had talons unlike any beast, monster, or creature I have seen
Those from my wildest nightmares wouldn't compare
For those claws has no limit of in entanglements, distance, or damage to induced
I struggled with such foolery so much deceiving demeanor and undermining intentions

I didn't know I could see the day where sirens don't see in her presence
Even to those feast on the hearts and desires of men from the depths of hell
Stays silent moved aside with grace from her

I watch,
As she took what I loved from me
Destroying the one thing I truly cared about

Breaking him down into less of a man
Did you know when a person truly dies?
When their spirit is broken
I see the slate gray pigmented eyes
The frozen face of despair
A heart that no longer cares

I couldn't move
Run
Jog
Or even scream too
The man I loved and knew
Forgot about me too

I hold him in my arms
Begging him to notice me
To return the color of life
To his emotionless body
Whispers to me,
"I'm okay, honey."

That day-
A piece inside of me died and knew
I would always love you

Purgatory

Walking in circles
Same choices and mistakes
An endless loop of utter chaotic behavior
Always looking over the left shoulder
Second to Third
Fourth to Fifth
Chances?

Sorry becomes redundant
Losing the apologetic meaning
Like how feeling invisible to the world
Thoughts, feelings, morals are now irrelevant
A vision of others warped
But, Denial is a disease

Plagues the mind
With shackles and concrete
Feeling trapped, shut off
Dead ends and Cutoffs
Numb to the abuse
Able to hear echo screams of cries for help
Trapped in the mindset
Similar to hell

You have no control

Here alone and nowhere else to go
As existence grows faint
Fading due to the mistake
This mistake was the belief of everything being
TO LATE

Better

She fights the feeling of loneliness one more time, trying to catch her breath
The fear of rejection and the unknown consumes her mind
Her screams which were faint weeks ago, have now become a forever cycle of a horrific uproar
Her mind with an exact image of herself in a room full of mirrors of herself
She sees the memories of herself, showing the morals and self-respect she once had for herself
Bashing, kicking, screaming, and crawling her way through his wicked sin that plagued her thoughts
She couldn't escape his grasp
The promises that he now denied being apart of
Of a better time, better life, and a better person
Now all she would wish for is for him to listen
Hear her plea for help
What he gave her was silence
She didn't want to be engulfed, and it wasn't warming
The doubts and fear began to feast of her mindset
As she became as cold as the chill that haunts an empty room

He rushes in, bashing his fist into the wall
She stood in pure disbelief horror
The promises and love shattered right in front of her
Every smile and blushing face tainted with the terror that surrounds her
Closing her eyes, rapidly over & over again
Trying to escape the nightmare she believes to be in
His fist covered in blood, turning to look at her
She was frozen
The shackles from the image of what her lover currently painting wouldn't ever be forgotten
Utter disbelief of what she believed was real wasn't as true as she had once knew
He stood there, the color of rage covered his angered face
Lifting up his crimson covered fist, he looked at the wounds more carefully
Her gulp echoed the room as she slowly walked towards him
She ripped a strip from her dress to cover the burdens now engraved into his skin
As his fist was covered in scars, so was her heart
Attempting to rekindle what bridge had been burnt, something in her changed that night
A fresh breeze blew the ashes away
She lived each day happily from that

To believe in a fairy tale to turn into a nightmare never forgotten
Morals are always there, reality or not
Forgive but not forgotten

Ash

She was the color of eternal rage
She attacked with a blitz of engulfing crimson flames
The horns were a sign of pure evil
The scales showed she was a horrific monster
She was an enteral nightmare
She was the mere beast who plagued the lands with her hatred
"I'll shed my scales of all the burdens I have carried. Washes the insanity from my skin. To show the beauty within."
Her words of enlightenment spoke in a blaze of embers
She soars above any man's expectations
The horns she wore spoke with age and wisdom
The scales she engraved with spoke of hardships and conquest
She was sized her ambitions
If for the one who is seeking her
She lies just above the mountains, behind the waterfall of sorrow tears and surrounding the willows that symboled her inside dormant feelings
What everyone saw was negative to her

The truth is very harmful to those who are uneducated and not open-minded
She has seen much for the age she is that gave her life experience
She was thick-skinned due to the negative people and harmful words
She has stars in her eyes, dreams bigger than herself
You see, even if she was the Dragon she was meant to be,
The Dragon's heart is the weakest part
So there wasn't much of a difference between her and me
The weakest part of a human is the heart

Cheated

Such beauty once upon a time eluded me
I caressed your face, told you that you were the
only one
The now-vacant whispers of candied nothings
echoed throughout my mind

Such deception you placed into me
To color our future with such fiction
Such a myth to believe I was the man for you,
wasn't it?
Gaslighting me into the fabrication that it was
me, not you
I would obstruct in a panic on what next to say
to you.

The examination of myself as a man
I would query with peers, friends, family.
Somehow they would say maybe so it couldn't
have been you.
Wondering how someone as such beauty could
orchestrate the control entirely of someone's life

It cheated me out of my sanity
The exaggerations you would spread to basis
minds.

The trepidation you promised me you wouldn't
inflect slowly became my reality.
Why him?
Why allow me to combine to believe once
manhood into falsehood?
He didn't just occupy my bed or my wife,
Such insubstantial morals and integrity,
He occupies expectations of what I believe was
the foundation of our lives to have been spent.

You gained such satisfaction to watch myself
suffer.
To become my burden delighted you.
Watching me survey the damage left upon me,
you were going with a smile
My torment was such ecstasy for you
How could someone have such contentment in
the agony they induced?
How did I ever become so disturbed by the one I
once loved?

To avoid my calls
To evade the truth to been told.
To dodge the dates, I made
To sidestep onward to the next guy.
To frustrate me, with me

You cheated
You cheated me
You cheated on me

Done

Goodbye or Gone
Competed or Terminated
Forgotten or Closure
Dumped or Ended
Empty or No More

The customary of being "Done."
When did goodbye and closure become not socially acceptable?
To better yourself and remain healthy, deem a sin?
To be listed as the wrong one-

Interest & Views are invalid.
My intentions are untrue or false.
My view of them, they said, is to be inaccurate and flawed.
The will or choice to say, "I'm Done."
Bogus,
Phony,
Dicey,
Or an easy way out, coward, they must say.

Erroneous, you're running from your issues-
No- I'm deemed flawed for self-awareness of my
mental health.

Here- is to everything; inappropriate I endured.
How I as a whole felt undesirable, but my logic
said it was ill-advised to have an opinion.
No, your indecorous values of me would be your
own unbecoming.
To see myself dissolve as a person,
My soul combust into ashes,
My heart to vanish within the emptiness of my
body,
My health diminishing within my prime,
My body decay into the soiled square you
framed for me,
Just so I am beyond the pale, from anyone's
touch.

As I ascend,
Levitate with grace to conquer my endeavors
No- I am not "Done."
To scale the unlimited possibilities of my
ambitions would be too modest of me.
I remain humble to my core.
But I loom with forgiveness to tower over those
who wanted me beneath them.
For when I say "Done," it is an exhilaration of
freedom.

I wish no ill-will but the satisfaction of bliss that glows on my face.
I wasn't nor am I to be contained,
it is for that I will see you remain within the narrow-minded mindset,
for the fact, you threat control with the use of what is "Done."

A Wallflower's Blessing

Sometimes she walks amongst everyone else, looking at the world with her curious stone hazel eyes.

But what she sees is the true beauty of life in this world. Every little soul, breath, and even smallest movement of the wind. She sees the good that lies within the edged scars and the bruised skin. But the most genuine feeling of pain lies within, just past the pale grey sorrowful eyes. The most painful truth is that there are no emotions inside. Most had little care if they lived or died, but the slightest touch from her skin to theirs gave the warmest feeling on the inside. She wasn't like most, and she was a wallflower that just watched and listened. But, just the slightest smile will give you the quickest healing. She was a beautiful soul, without a doubt.

She was in that rain when there was a drought. She was that breeze when on a hot summer day.

She was the first flower that bloomed in May.
She was snowing when the kids played.
She was the light in the darkest cave.

Though I may not even know her name, her eyes were the exact color of pale grey. However, she has been through the same pain. I just hoped for someone to touch her heart as she touched the world.

Clay

Self-image is something that everyone holds
standards in
The first impression is everything and defines
you as a person whether to believe in
But, life is like Clay
It's what you make of it
The burning passion for success is what makes it
concrete
No one but yourself is in control of your image
To what I look in the mirror truly a horrid
hollow mess
I feel the pains and truths of what is here in front
of me, only see through the burning bridges
before me
Those who have used me for my worth and
smiled in my face as they stood over me
But wasn't it me that hung and tied my noose
accordingly?
I choose to see the best in this world now,
Now my mind is a maelstrom of chaotic
thoughts
As I walk myself to the block
To be guillotined and swept away into what
oblivion I made for myself

Even when breathing, I stopped believing and drowned myself in this purgatory
To have history repeat itself, I wasn't as strong as you believe in
I am merely human..
But I was already dead upon meeting you.
You sentenced me to my death
This as premeditated murder of myself through your hands just began.
To watch me rip myself limb by limb to laugh and make myself listen to echoes of my sorrow..
You had me in the kill zone from day one
But, life is like Clay, it's what you make of it
The burning passion to succeed is what makes it concrete
I'm a melted mess..
To recover to reform is a blessing
I decide my fate or what path to take, I'm free of this mindset of self-hate
To believe in loving once more, or to close another door
This is another chapter that will pass once more,
So mote it be

Easer, Auto Correct, and the Backspace

I write with my heart and illustrate with my
mind
Everything I experience is in the first person, the
thoughts of my daily mindset
Just like my life is a daily diary or documentary
From what I speak on, it is truly from my heart
and influenced by my mind
Life isn't published until your gone
As your life develops into a book, that blossoms
into a third-person view
The characters you encounter, you don't know
their intentions or motives
Not everything is meant the last, just as the book
comes to an end
So I continue writing, but with a pencil only
To erase the negativity from me

Puddle

What if I looked at the puddle upside down,
would my reflection smile back at me? Or frown
up at me?
The disturbed tone in the watery mirror
can only show my appearance or the sorrowful
pain beneath it?
I wonder if I slammed my fist into the shudder,
would it show me something worth it?
Water can be in the shape of anything,
and with the smallest drop could end everything
I would assume with the metaphor at play that's
why we are this way
Free will of thinking, but plagued with the hate
enough to kill our kind

Stance

Today I was kicked in my mouth
Left as a stray
Invisible as it gets
Hey is nonexistent
I know I wasn't given a fair shake
But it was the deal that I made
Odds stacked against me
Everyone from the start knew they hated me
Set up to fail
They thought I would be starving, dead, or in jail
This story of my life I do come to tell
About how those who smile or silently compete
with you
Won't ever be the death of you
I'll lead the way
I'm a legend
The one you'll hear of every day

Rebellion

When did we place standards on the diversity of
people and ways of culture
When did we buy into emotionless propaganda
When did we sell our way of beliefs to social
media
We sold our voice, and with that, we lost our
purpose and freedom
Freedom of our thought process
I say slavery still exist
Enslaved to the thoughts and beliefs of what we
were told is right and wrong
Does everyone forget why America came to be
Dreams, desires, & diversity gave us culture and
traditions
We were family
When did we allow Fear > Respect
When did we allow such entitlement and
arrogance to plague our streets
We are equal
Everyone is entitled to breathe this air as much
as those left, right, behind, and in front of them
If we are to deny them, we're no different than
the hate we're fighting against
We lost our vision among this
Times change people change

We must educate over hate
Listen to understand and not to reply
Social media shackles limit our distance of understanding
What is a negative can become a positive
As fast as we spread viral hate, do questionable things for clout or clickbait
We can educate
Self-awareness is key in our mindset of forming opinions
Communication is key
During this time
Everyone is dropping to the ground for the smallest amount of optimism
Reputation, power, wealth shouldn't be a currency to determine someone's rights to live or be counted equal
Take notes of this-
This virus made us equal
It doesn't see fame, wealth, race, age, or sex
We are in an era where all the wrong things validate our life choices into what we believe to be "okay."
We became selfish
As these fires burn from the ambitions of willpower and fortitude
We are aware of no balance
Good / Bad

As we gain justice here- it should continue as such
But- bringing such harm to those, we are fist in the air against
Wouldn't do justice- we become the very hate we scream out against
We can't lose ourselves in this madness
Patience and consistency will become perseverance
We must not ever forget the vision we are fighting for
I feel this is far from over
But- we forge this path now, as the usage of mass communications we have access to now
We can reach massive volumes of understatement and speak accordingly on the choices we have made and yet to make
We have a voice
I have a voice
Now it's our choice
To use it wisely

Weight

I'm glad you're gone
A weight has been lifted from my chest and
mind
I am not fatigued anymore
I'm not questioning myself anymore
I don't feel haunted with those judging eyes
anymore
Basis views
Words misconstrued
Alter version of you
Sick of the thought of you
No anger
Only disgust
To the image and views of what you explained a
"US"
One-sided
Narrow-minded
I laugh now
The belief of such entitlement awareness you
thought you had
0 here, and would be 0 anywhere else
You're not one to control the actions of
someone's choice
Believing you owned my trust

What, because of the definition of what you believe is "Love."
Calling someone's culture, transitions, and lifestyles a waste
Baffled by the true colors of envy on your face
To hold someone down to drown for you to stay afloat
Above the line of what is an "Advantage."
Say you're hopelessly romantic
But, to court every girl who caress you
Fed on their kindness
Mother told me, "Takers live better, but Givers sleep better."
I'm judged on a social standard defined by what love is
Yet, told I am not good enough
But it's I, but you
I can't say I was yours
When you weren't mind
This weight released from me
I see clearly
I'm glad I wasn't ever yours
Used to being alone
Alpha to the pack
The "Well Together" one
Voted most likely to be successful in high school
To the bliss of your own achievements, the face of your loved ones

You still feel as such of haunting chill in the room of your peers
Those proud of you are quick to disregard you due to time as an inconvenience
Said you care, said you were proud
Bragged on my achievements into the faces of strangers
Accepting and lucky you say
Thankful to have me?
Here I am, to be scolded for what makes me feel empowered and beautiful
Healthy colorful mindset
Unfit to those with selfish intentions
Judged on worth due to someone's demands of social interaction and social society image
No wrong way of life
But, "Optimism" is rare with the traits of understanding trust
Loyalty, trust, communication practiced in compromise
But, this is a formal was of expression and my last and final goodbye

Intimacy

Struggling with an image painted with pain and anger
Surrounded by a group of my peers
To jump, kick, or stream out
Do you notice my suffering?
With beauty comes pain, people say?
Comfortability, I add,
To be open, exposed, naked, and scared
To be comforted with the trusted embrace of warmth within
Only selective times, I felt heard
Am I a convenience?

Wanted only with a 2nd handed desire?
Speak up, he said
It was he that didn't answer
This leads me to question, is there a right or wrong way to this?
Am I wrong to feel the way I do?
Would it have been acceptable to speak up?
It would ruin his happiness, I thought
What if he finds it within the embrace of someone else?
Would this be my fault?
Be my fault as a convenience?

Independence Day

Today I felt a piece of me die within the inside
As another piece felt liberated within me
A new type of independence born
The same day of America
Oh the irony
The same belief of being true to oneself
Having the freedom to do and believe in
anything you desire
Believing in yourself and falling in love with
yourself all over again
Seeing your image in the mirror
Expressing the emotions that you buried inside
that inspired the screams within your mind
Like fireworks-
The amount of heat and pressure causes an
explosion
Like a situation that breaks within us- we burst
to feel ourselves again
Beautiful and bright-minded
With the fizzles being whimsical in the sky
We realize much to achieve
Like the song written in the glory
This is our song to believe in achieving what
could be

The End

Silence to anyone can make or break a person's will.
Silence can help one reconcile with one's inner being.
But, I wouldn't dare wish loneliness onto someone.
With loneliness comes a pain to which it could break the strongest person down.
The gentle whispers of doubt and regret can plague one's mind.
It starts as the unnoticed, the feeling of being invisible to the world.
The silence of the world allows you to question your existence.
You come home to an empty house of people who can't remember who you are.
You begin to think, as you see smiling faces go past you, "Am I better off dead?"
The worst part is being dead to the people you care for.
Nightmares spoke with vivid imagery..

"I woke up in a hospital because I was in a coma, and after waking up, I learned I lost everything, my career, my family no longer remembered me, all of my friends, and worst of all you. I remembered it all, but when I tried to come around it as if I was living a lie as if I existed in a world where I was the ultimate outcast or completely unknown. Everyone looked at me like I was a stranger and couldn't progress my relations with anyone whatsoever. Everything or everyone my heart belonged to that I tried to come in contact with just turned to ash in front of me and took some of me with it. Then those I didn't associate with laughed at me and ridiculed me as they watched me slowly die of a broken heart and a scorched memory. As time went by, I aged faster than anyone else, growing old and decaying knowing I couldn't watch my children grow up or enjoy my life with someone I eventually ended right where I woke up the first time and was sentenced to death by whom I cherished from the pain of heartache."

Dreams are in the mere forms of wake up calls,
Or deep desires.
Don't let the silence come before your curtain call.
This loneliness
is the silence before the end.

www.ingramcontent.com/pod-product-compliance
Lightning Source LLC
Chambersburg PA
CBHW051746130826
49812CB00033B/1025
* 9 7 8 9 3 5 7 2 1 3 2 8 8 *